My World of Science

BENDY
AND RIGID

Angela Royston

Heinemann Library
Chicago, Illinois

Customer Service 888-454-2279

Visit our website at www.heinemannlibrary.com

Designed by Jo Hinton-Malivoire and Tinstar Design Limited
Originated by Blenheim Colour, Ltd.
Printed and bound in China by South China Printing Company
Photo research by Maria Joannou and Sally Smith

07 06 05 04
10 9 8 7 6 5 4 3 2

Library of Congress Cataloging-in-Publication Data
Royston, Angela.
    Bendy and rigid / Angela Royston.
      p. cm. – (My world of science)
    Summary: Provides a simple explanation of the physical prop-
  erties of rigid and flexible objects, including examples of their
  uses in nature and everyday life.
    Includes bibliographical references and index.
    ISBN 1-40340-858-0 (HC), 1-40343-171-X (Pbk)
    1. Flexure–Juvenile literature.   [1. Flexure.]   I. Title.
  II. Series: Royston, Angela. My world of science.
  TA417.7.F5R69 2003
  620.1'123–dc21

  2002009400

Acknowledgments
The author and publishers are grateful to the following for permission to reproduce copyright material:
pp. 4, 5, 6, 7, 10, 11, 13, 14, 15, 16, 18, 19, 21, 22, 23, 27, 28 Trevor Clifford; p. 8 Rupert Horrox; pp. 9, 29 Chris Fairclough/Eye Ubiquitous; p. 12 Powerstock/ZEFA; p. 17 PhotoDisc; pp. 20, 25 Getty Images; p. 24 David Bradford; p. 26 Chris Honeywell.

Cover photograph by Trevor Clifford.

Some words are shown in bold, **like this.** You can find out what they mean by looking in the glossary.

Contents

What Is Bendy? 4

How Much Does It Bend? 6

What Is Rigid? 8

How Rigid Is It? 10

Plastic 12

Wheels 14

Shoes 16

Paper and Cardboard 18

Thick and Thin 20

Bending and Breaking 22

Wood Can Bend 24

Porcelain Is Brittle 26

Other Brittle Materials 28

Glossary 30

More Books to Read 31

Index 32

What Is Bendy?

This toy snake is bendy. You can twist it into different shapes. Here the snake is bent into the shape of the letter "S."

This girl is trying on a belt. She bends it around her waist and through the belt buckle. A rigid belt would not work at all!

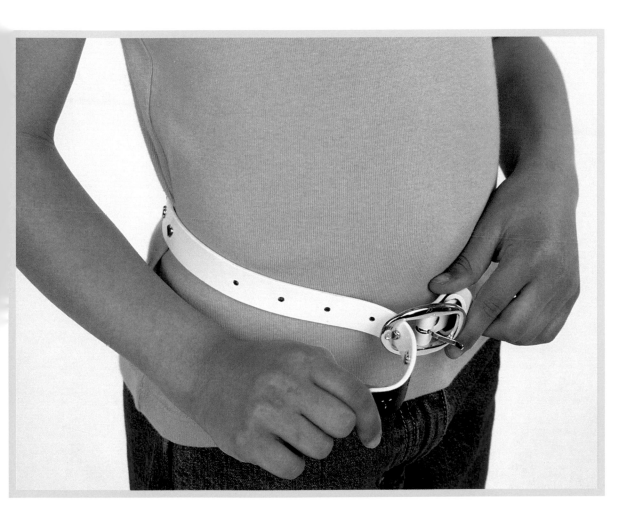

How Much Does It Bend?

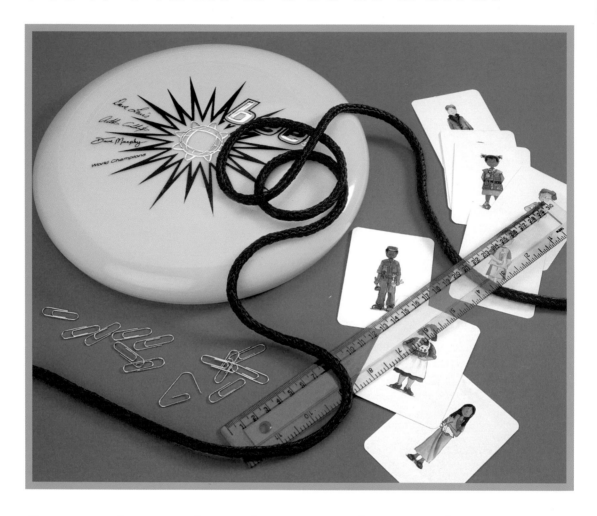

Some things bend more than others.
The playing cards bend more than
the ruler. But the rope bends more
than all the other things.

Objects that look the same can bend differently. Some shoes bend more than others. These children want to find out whose shoe bends the most.

What Is Rigid?

This **xylophone** is rigid. You cannot change its shape by bending it. However much you push or pull, it keeps the same shape.

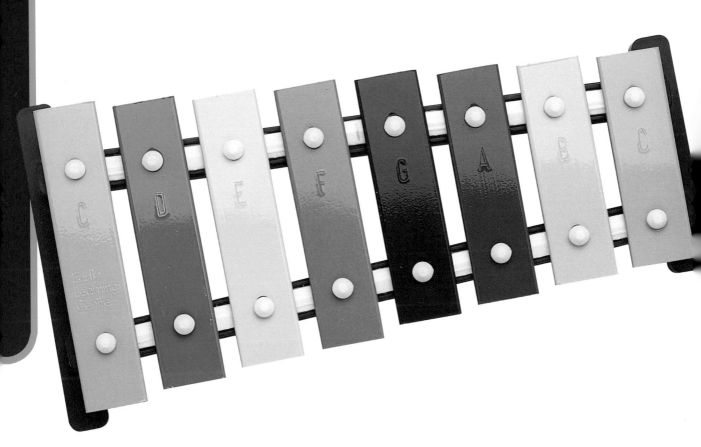

The pan and the plate are both rigid. This is a good thing! If they were bendy, your food would fall off them.

How Rigid Is It?

A ruler is rigid. It will keep its shape unless you bend it. Even then, the ruler will only bend a little bit.

The **screwdriver** is more rigid than the ruler. But the most rigid thing here is the tile. It will not bend at all.

Plastic

Some plastic can bend. This raincoat is made of bendy plastic. It is easy to put on and move around in.

This plastic **garden hose** bends a lot. You can even wind it into a circle. But the watering can is rigid. That is why it can hold water.

Wheels

Bicycle wheels have **rubber** tires. Rubber is strong and bendy. It will bend when you go over a bump.

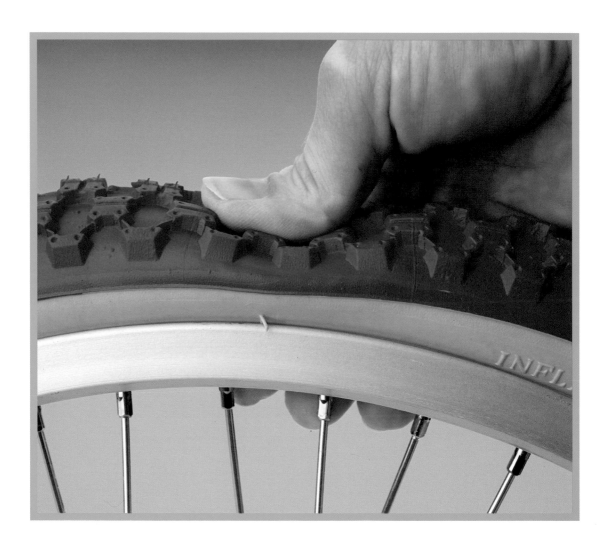

A bicycle wheel has a rigid **rim** and **spokes.** They hold the tire in place. The tire would not hold its shape without the rim and spokes.

Shoes

Shoes bend as you walk. This lets you bend your feet. The bottoms of shoes are made of strong plastic or **leather.**

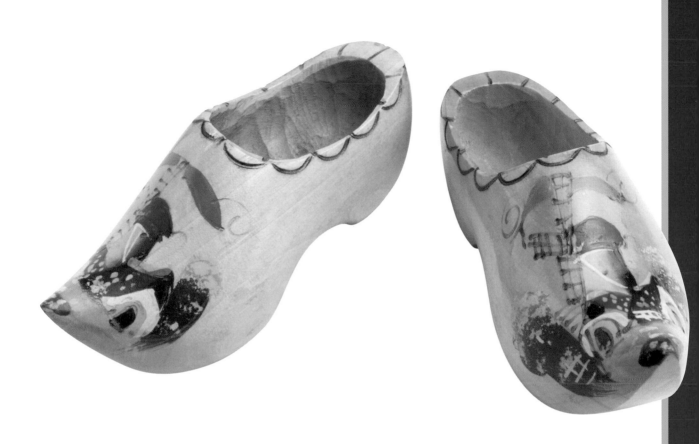

These shoes are called **clogs.**
They are made of rigid wood. The
wood does not bend as you walk.
It is not very easy to walk in clogs!

Paper and Cardboard

A sheet of paper bends a lot. It can be rolled or folded. Then you can unroll or unfold the paper to make it flat.

This box is made of cardboard. It is more rigid than paper. This is because cardboard is thick. Cardboard makes strong, rigid boxes.

Thick and Thin

Thin objects bend more than thick objects. These thick steel **beams** will not bend easily. They make a rigid frame for a building.

These paper clips are made of steel, just like the beams. But the paper clips are thin. This makes them easy to bend.

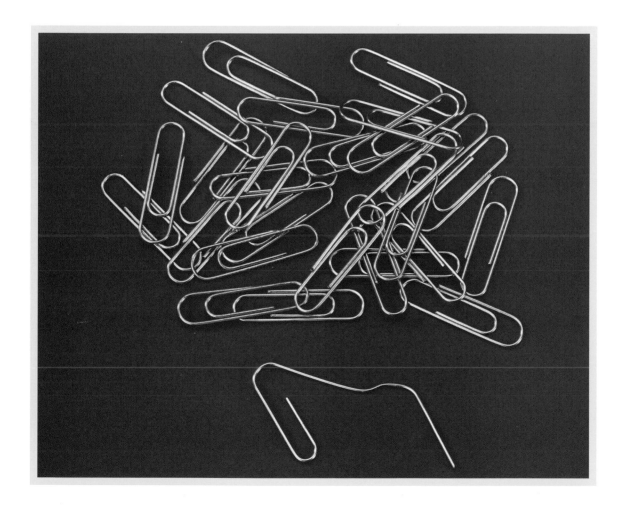

Bending and Breaking

Some things only bend a little. Then they break. This woman bent the stick until it broke into two pieces.

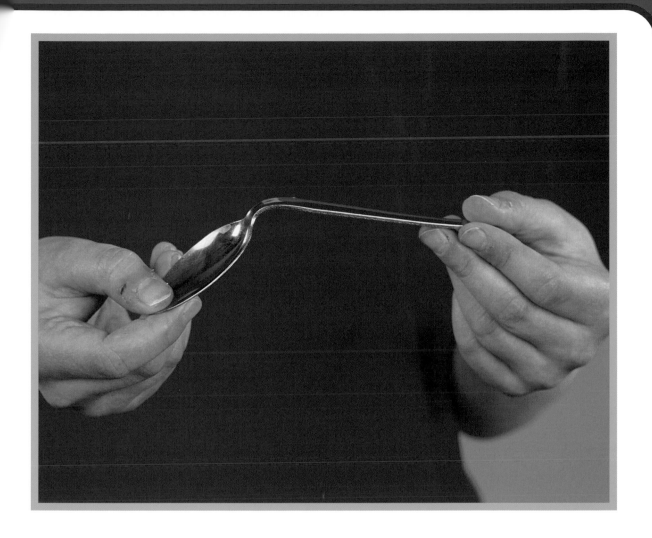

Some things bend a few times before they break. If this spoon is bent over and over again, it will break.

Wood Can Bend

Sometimes wood can bend. The cat's basket is made from wooden **twigs.** The twigs are bent and twisted together.

Most tree **trunks** have wood inside.
The bendy wood keeps them from
blowing over. The winds of a **hurricane**
are bending these palm trees.

Porcelain Is Brittle

Some rigid things, such as these **porcelain** cups and saucers, are **brittle.** This means that it is easy to crack or break them.

Porcelain is used to make many plates, bowls, and vases. Be careful not to drop porcelain! It may break.

Other Brittle Materials

Most glass is more **brittle** than **porcelain.** These glasses are very thin. They can break or crack easily.

Stones and bricks are brittle, too. But they are very thick. They do not break easily. This worker is breaking the stone with a **sledgehammer.**

Glossary

beam thick piece of steel used to hold up a building

brittle easy to break into pieces

clog shoe made of wood

garden hose long tube used to carry water to a garden

hurricane storm that produces strong winds and heavy rain

leather material made from the skin of a cow or other animal

porcelain material used to make plates, bowls, cups, and vases

rim round, rigid part of a wheel on a bicycle or car

rubber bendy material made from rubber trees

screwdriver tool used to put screws into wood and other materials

sledgehammer big, heavy hammer

spokes thin rods that join the rim of a wheel to the center

trunk thickest part of a tree

twig small branch

xylophone musical instrument with wooden bars

More Books to Read

Madgwick, Wendy. *Super Materials.* Austin, Tex.: Raintree Publishers, 1999.

Oxlade, Chris. *Plastic.* Chicago: Heinemann Library, 2001.

Riley, Peter. *Materials and Processes.* Danbury, Conn.: Scholastic Library Publishing, 1999.

Index

bending and breaking 22–23

bendy objects 4–7

brittle materials 26–29

cardboard 19

glass 28

paper 18, 19

plastic 12–13

porcelain 26–27

rigid objects 8–11

shoes 7, 16–17

stone 29

thick materials 20

thin materials 21

wheels 14–15

wood 24–25